In
SEARCH
of DEITIES

FANTASIES OF THE SIX DYNASTIES

搜神记

ILLUSTRATED BY | TRANSLATED BY
WANG XUANMING | **CLARA SHOW**

ASIAPAC • SINGAPORE

Publisher
ASIAPAC BOOKS PTE LTD
629 Aljunied Road #04-06
Cititech Industrial Building
Singapore 1438
Tel: 7453868
Fax: 7453822

First published September 1994

© ASIAPAC BOOKS, 1994
ISBN 981-3029-35-8

Cover design by Bay Song Lin
Typeset by Unistar Graphics Pte Ltd
Body text in 8/9 pt Helvetica
Printed in Singapore by
Loi Printing Pte Ltd

Publisher's Note

Man has always been fascinated by the supernatural and the "other" world. There are countless books and films on this topic alone. Since ancient times, many such stories of gods, spirits, immortality, etc, were written or handed down verbally from generation to generation.

We are proud to present *In Search of Deities,* the first book in this new series on Myths and Legends. Comprising various supernatural and bizarre tales from the Six Dynasties, *In Search of Deities* contains many invaluable moral messages subtly dispensed through the creative hand of Wang Xuanming, a contemporary cartoonist from China, who has already illustrated a highly popular series of ancient Chinese military classics.

We would like to thank Wang Xuanming for allowing us to publish his best-selling comics in English, Clara Show for translating this volume and the production team for putting in their best effort in the publication of this book.

About the Editor/Illustrator

Wang Xuanming, a contemporary cartoonist in China, was born in Beijing in 1950. He was trained formally in commercial art and industrial art. Since 1972, he has been engaged in various aspects of artistic work, even undertaking the production of screen advertisements and artistic stage designs. Wang's contribution to the field of art is immense. He frequently explores various ways of expressing his artistic talents. Besides a lot of cartoons, picture books, and illustrations, he also does oil paintings and posters. His works have on many occasions entered nationwide art exhibitions, won awards in several art competitions, and have been selected for inclusion in various art albums.

Wang's cartoons, illustrations, and other works have been serialized in all the major newspapers and publications in Beijing since 1980. His cartoons entitled *Different Gravitational Force* is praised by famous Chinese artists, and was selected for inclusion in the *Anthology of Chinese Scientific Cartoons*. In 1987, he participated in the creation of the animated cartoon *Brother Elephant*, which captured the hearts of many children when it was first shown on television.

Wang has worked with many publishers in Beijing, such as China Friendly Publishing Co., Chinese Cultural Publishing Co., Huaxia Publishing Co., People's Art Publishing Co., and Zhaohua Publishing Co. He has gained the trust and confidence of both publishers and artists alike.

In his *Books of Strategy* comic series, he uses a simple and humorous art form to introduce ancient Chinese military classics to modern readers. The books were very well received by people from all walks of life when they were first published in China; the Beijing Radio Station made a special interview of this series of books and highly recommended it to the public. This series is published by China Friendly Publishing Co. in China, and by Treasure Creation Co. Ltd. in Hongkong. Asiapac Books in Singapore is the publisher for the English edition of this series.

Wang is at present an art editor at the *China Science and Technology Daily*.

Preface

Some scholars divide the wide spectrum of ancient Chinese novels into three categories: historic epics like *Romance of the Three Kingdoms*; romance classics like *Dream of the Red Mansions*; and mythical fantasies like *Journey to the West*. These scholars are of the opinion that of the three types, mythical fantasies are the forerunners of Chinese novels. As to whether there is any validity in this, I will not comment as I have not made any in-depth study in this area. However, mythical fantasies do, undoubtedly, occupy an important spot in Chinese culture.

The development of mythical fantasies peaked during the period from the Qin dynasty to the Wei, Jin, Southern and Northern dynasties. During this time, there was a surge of new ideas and abundant supply of authors. Numerous collections of stories sprang up, among which, *In Search of Deities* was the most representative. It was to have a great impact on the works which blossomed in later generations.

In Search of Deities was compiled by Gan Bao, a native of Henan. He was first commissioned by Emperor Yuan of the Jin dynasty to compile and write the history of the era. His work won him the admiration and praise of many a historian. He then went on to compile *In Search of Deities*.

Gan Bao lived in an unusual era in Chinese history - the Wei, Jin, Southern and Northern dynasties. This period fell between the Qin, Han dynasties and the Sui, Tang dynasties which were economically and culturally vibrant during their times. The Wei, Jin, Southern and Northern dynasties which lasted some 400 years were marked by civil strife. Due to social unrest, there was widespread movement of people from one place to another. This eventually gave rise to new ideas in production skills which in turn boosted the economy throughout the empire. Scholars in the cultural field, stifled by Confucianism which monopolised the culture climate, began to search for freer modes of expression. Consequently, there was a hub of activity in the area of literary creations. *In Search of Deities* was compiled under these circumstances.

Ancient China was characterized by popular deity worshipping. Through imagination, people created numerous deities and spirits. The origins, formation and development of mythical fantasies was a complicated but interesting process. People gave names to deities and spirits. They believed they existed everywhere - in heaven, in hell and on earth. Their beliefs provided a rich and interesting source of ideas for authors.

Though some of the contents in the fairy tales seemed far-fetched and ludicrous at times, it was not quite so. The authors had a more important mission in conveying moral messages through the plots. More often than not, the stories reflect the author's feelings and philosophy; and draw the reader's attention to the good and flip side of mankind. For example, in *In Search of Deities*, Gan Bao was dispensing moral messages while telling stories of the supernatural. Though most of the characters in his stories possess some incredible power or other, they were not lacking in feelings and thoughts, be they good or evil. Whether the deities or spirits dwelled in heaven or hell, they were intricately linked with man. These elements of romance, mystery and suspense contributed substantially to the artistic charm of Gan Bao's work.

I sincerely hope that readers will, through this book, learn to appreciate the essence of ancient Chinese literature and along the way, realize the true meaning of life.

Wang Xuanming

Translator's Note

How many of us remember our childhood when we were told mystery stories that had simple plots but which fascinated and kept us in suspense? *In Search of Deities* is one such collection of tales that does not boast of complicated story lines or dramatic endings. Its unpretentious plots could perhaps be traced to its origins as part of the Chinese narrative genre known as *Zhi Guai* (*Records of Anomalies*). Produced during the Six Dynasties, these stories were circulated verbally. Hence, it was essential that characters were kept to the minimum and story line, brief and uncluttered to enable listeners to follow the developments without difficulty.

The main objectives of the stories were to entertain and educate. In *The Beast-Man*, the story begins with the capture of a man who turned out to be a tiger. The underlying message which readers gather at the end of it is: we cannot be too cautious of devious characters around us who, more often than not, go about with life acting like decent people. *Zhang Pu Keeps His Word* tells the importance of sticking to one's promises. However, the moral messages are dispensed subtly, not forced down the reader's throat.

Of course, there are also tales on the evergreen themes of love and loyalty which never fail to touch the hearts of even the sceptics amongst us. Other stories deal with gods, ghosts and spirits. Despite their no-fuss plots, the elements of suspense and surprise are still there. Avid readers of mysteries, accustomed to complicated characterizations and plot within plot story lines may find this collection a refreshing change. For the rest of us, it is just reminiscence of the good old days when we read a mystery or heard a strange tale somewhere which we were able to recall details vividly from the beginning to the end.

Clara Show

Clara Show is a freelance translator.

Contents

The Supreme One Of Mount Jiao

焦 山 老 君

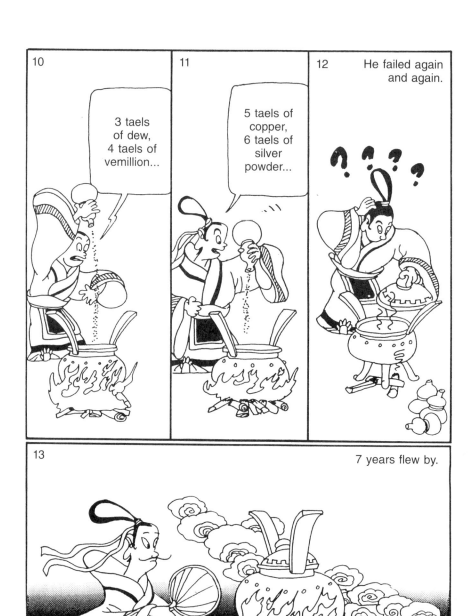

6

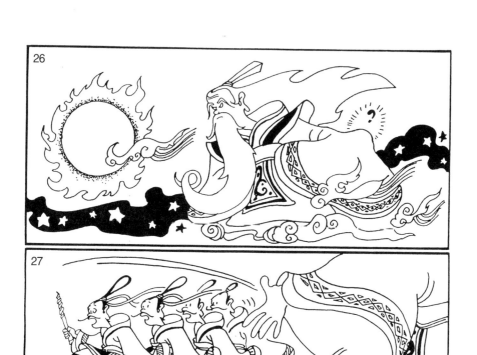

This boulder is 1,000 years old.

I want you to use the wooden drill to drill a hole through it.

11

Zuo Ci's Magic Skills

左 慈 使 神 通

15 Fantastic!

16 Then Cao Cao said:

Another one would be just nice.

17 I can easily fish for another.

I'll cook these personally, but I need ginger from Sichuan.

18

17

23

67 Cao Cao was outwitted again.

The Magic Of Ge Xuan
葛 玄 施 法

13

Ge Xuan dropped several copper coins into the well.

14

Come back to me!

15

What are those men doing?

16

One day, Ge Xuan was chatting with King Wu.

35

Zhang Pu Keeps His Word
張璞守信

1 The governor of Wu prefecture, Zhang Pu, was summoned to the capital by the Imperial Court. On his way there, he passed by Mount Lu.

2 His daughter and her maid decided to take a walk near the shrine.

4 Hee! Hee!

40

18 · The junk was still unable to move.

19 Looks like we have to throw Missy into the water.

20 I can't put everyone's life in danger just because of one person.

43

Gu Yezi

古 冶 子

Lord Qijing and his entourage were crossing the river when...

1

2

48

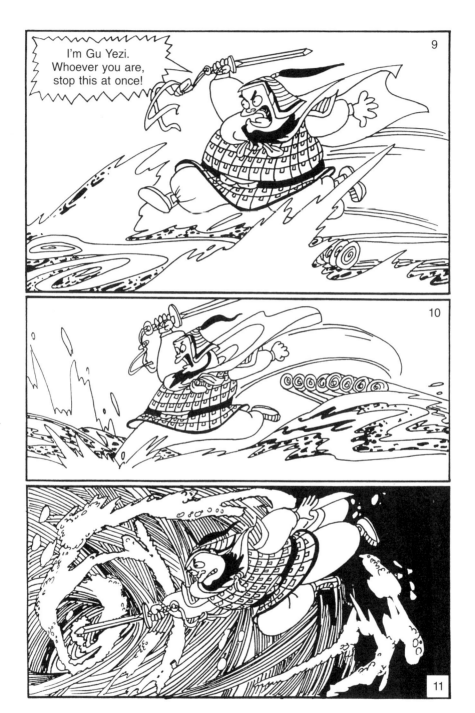

Gu Yezi ran across the rocks
in the middle of the river.

The Headless Jia Yong
賈雍無頭

1 During the reign of Emperor Wu of Han dynasty, the governor of Yuzhang prefecture, Jia Yong, led an army of soldiers to fight against the enemy troops.

2

3 Attack!

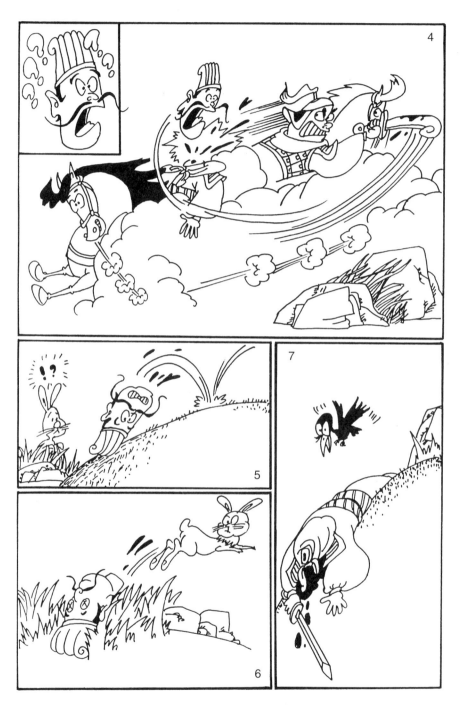

56

The headless Jia Yong mounted his horse and returned to the army camp.

58

Alien From Outer Space
星外來客

62

The state of Wu will be destroyed soon. Power will go to the Sima clan.

11

12

The children ran home and told their parents.

13

The people rushed to see the strange person that the children were talking about.

The Bizarre Pregnancy
飲 水 有 妊

5

6

Bring me that basin of water.

7

What does she want it for?

8

9

To everyone's horror, the boy turned into a puddle of water.

Cleaning The Coat With Fire

火 浣 單 衫

According to the ancient books, Kunlun was at the uppermost tip on earth.

Situated on top of Mount Kunlun was the Heavenly Emperor's capital on earth. It was a magnificent place.

To stop people from going up the mountain, the Heavenly Emperor surrounded it with water which not even a feather could float on.

The Lovelorn Tree
相 思 樹

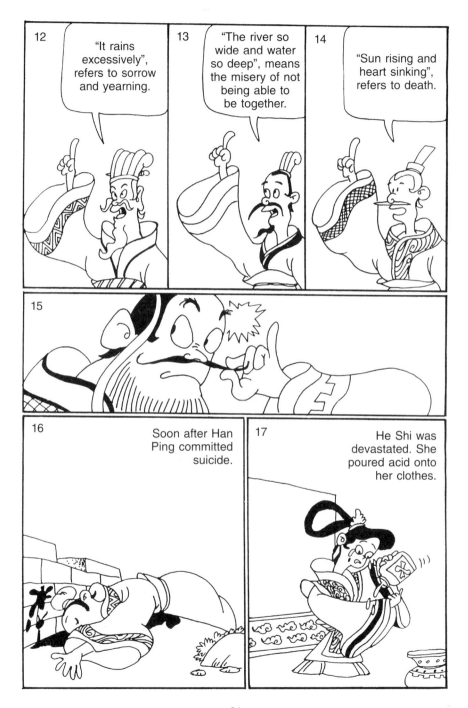

84

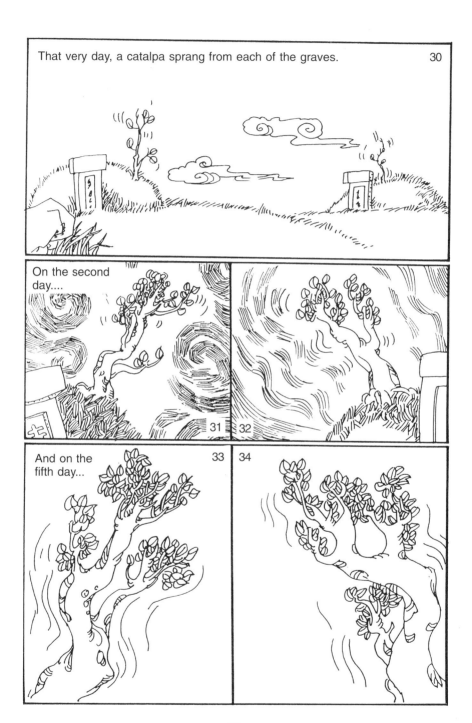

That very day, a catalpa sprang from each of the graves.

30

On the second day....

31 32

And on the fifth day...

33 34

86

Turning Beans Into Soldiers

撒 豆 成 兵

90

91

The beans turned into armed soldiers.

94

Fall Of The
Thunder God

霹靂落地

97

1   Yang Daohe was a farmer who lived during the Jin dynasty.

2

3   It started to rain and he quickly sought shelter under a mulberry tree.

98

Yang Daohe was attacked by thunderbolts.

102

Liu Gen
Summons
The Spirits

劉 根 召 鬼

106

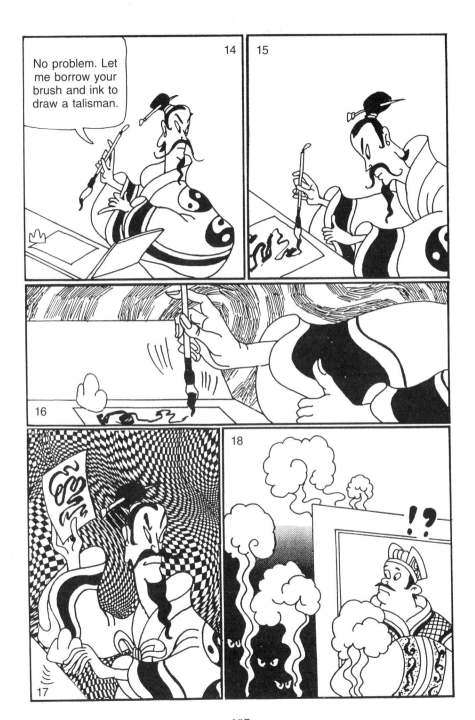

30 Not only did you fail to bring glory to our family, you offended a god and got us into trouble!

31

32

33

34 I made a terrible mistake…

35 Liu Gen left quietly and nobody knew where he had gone.

36 The spirits disappeared too.

The Beast-Man
貙人化虎

1. The people living in the region of River Han in Changjiang built a wooden cage to trap tigers.

2. As soon as an animal enters the cage, the door will slam shut.

3. Even the most aggressive tiger won't be able to escape.

4. We'll come back tomorrow to check the cage.

5. *Bang!* That very night, the cage door slammed shut.

116

117

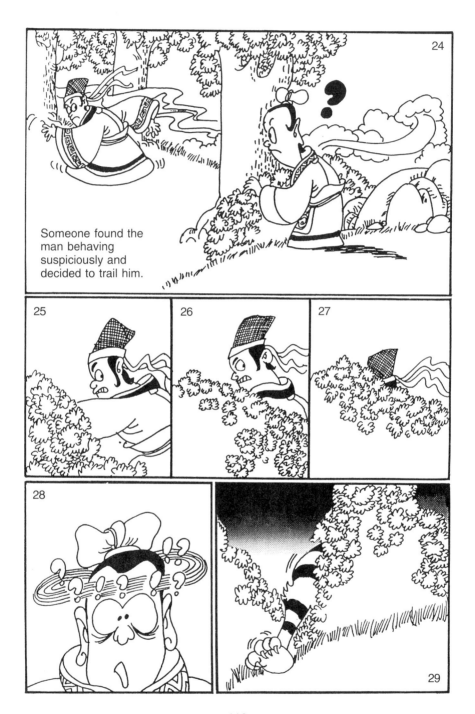

Someone found the man behaving suspiciously and decided to trail him.

118

The Golden Dragon Pond

金 龍 池

124

125

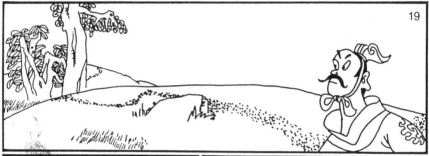

Start building along the gray path.

Very soon, the construction of Pingyang town was completed.

128

Wang Daoping's Wife

王 道 平 妻

134

135

138

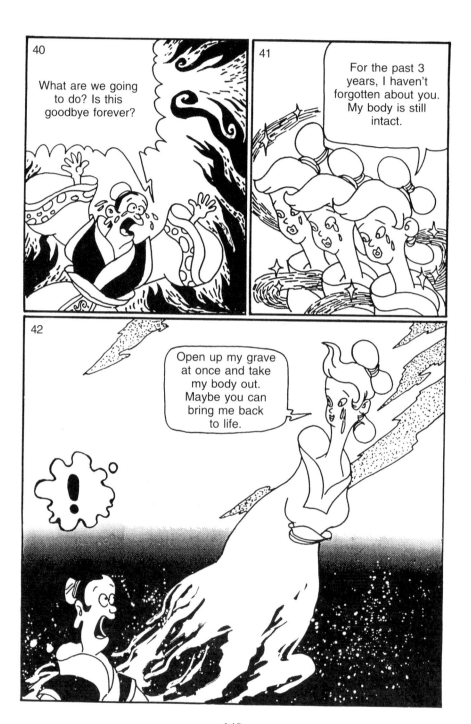

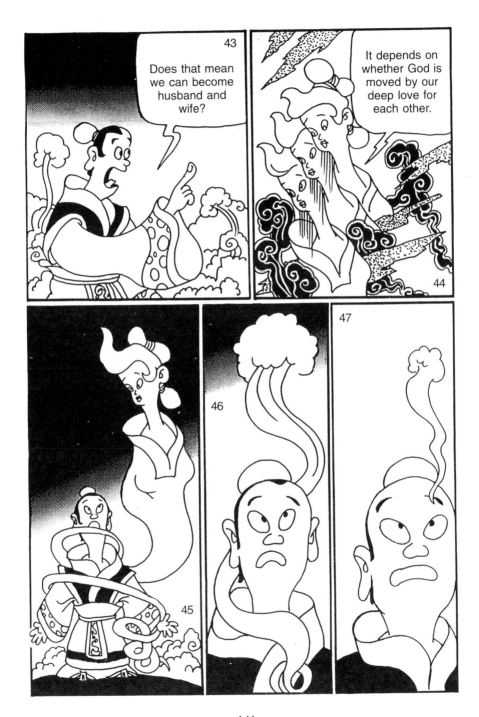

141

143

146

70 Liu Xiang was enraged when he found out.

Fuyu is my wife. How could she marry Wang Daoping?

71 Your Honour, please help me!

72 The magistrate went through all the scrolls on the country's rules and regulations.

There isn't any rule that covers that kind of situation.

73 Heaven was touched by the couple's love for each other. That's why the girl came back to life.

A Brief Chronology of Chinese History

夏 Xia Dynasty			About 2100 – 1600 BC
商 Shang Dynasty			About 1600 – 1100 BC
周 Zhou Dynasty	西周 Western Zhou Dynasty		About 1100 – 771 BC
	東周 Eastern Zhou Dynasty		770 – 256 BC
	春秋 Spring and Autumn Period		770 – 476 BC
	戰國 Warring States		475 – 221 BC
秦 Qin Dynasty			221 – 207 BC
漢 Han Dynasty	西漢 Western Han		206 BC – AD 24
	東漢 Eastern Han		25 – 220
三國 Three Kingdoms	魏 Wei		220 – 265
	蜀漢 Shu Han		221 – 263
	吳 Wu		222 – 280
西晉 Western Jin Dynasty			265 – 316
東晉 Eastern Jin Dynasty			317 – 420
南北朝 Northern and Southern Dynasties	南朝 Southern Dynasties	宋 Song	420 – 479
		齊 Qi	479 – 502
		梁 Liang	502 – 557
		陳 Chen	557 – 589
	北朝 Northern Dynasties	北魏 Northern Wei	386 – 534
		東魏 Eastern Wei	534 – 550
		北齊 Northern Qi	550 – 577
		西魏 Western Wei	535 – 556
		北周 Northern Zhou	557 – 581
隋 Sui Dynasty			581 – 618
唐 Tang Dynasty			618 – 907
五代 Five Dynasties	後梁 Later Liang		907 – 923
	後唐 Later Tang		923 – 936
	後晉 Later Jin		936 – 946
	後漢 Later Han		947 – 950
	後周 Later Zhou		951 – 960
宋 Song Dynasty	北宋 Northern Song Dynasty		960 – 1127
	南宋 Southern Song Dynasty		1127 – 1279
遼 Liao Dynasty			916 – 1125
金 Jin Dynasty			1115 – 1234
元 Yuan Dynasty			1271 – 1368
明 Ming Dynasty			1368 – 1644
清 Qing Dynasty			1644 – 1911
中華民國 Republic of China			1912 – 1949
中華人民共和國 People's Republic of China			1949 –

Strategy & Leadership Series by Wang Xuanming

Thirty-six Stratagems: Secret Art of War
Translated by Koh Kok Kiang (cartoons) &
Liu Yi (text of the stratagems)
A Chinese military classic which emphasizes deceptive schemes to achieve military objectives. It has attracted the attention of military authorities and general readers alike.

Six Strategies for War: The Practice of Effective Leadership
Translated by Alan Chong
A powerful book for rulers, administrators and leaders, it covers critical areas in management and warfare including: how to recruit talents and manage the state; how to beat the enemy and build an empire; how to lead wisely; and how to manoeuvre brilliantly.

Gems of Chinese Wisdom: Mastering the Art of Leadership
Translated by Leong Weng Kam
Wise up with this delightful collection of tales and anecdotes on the wisdom of great men and women in Chinese history, including Confucius, Meng Changjun and Gou Jian.

Three Strategies of Huang Shi Gong: The Art of Government
Translated by Alan Chong
Reputedly one of man's oldest monograph on military strategy, it unmasks the secrets behind brilliant military manoeuvres, clever deployment and control of subordinates, and effective government.

100 Strategies of War: Brilliant Tactics in Action
Translated by Yeo Ai Hoon
The book captures the essence of extensive military knowledge and practice, and explores the use of psychology in warfare, the importance of building diplomatic relations with the enemy's neighbours, the use of espionage and reconnaissance, etc.

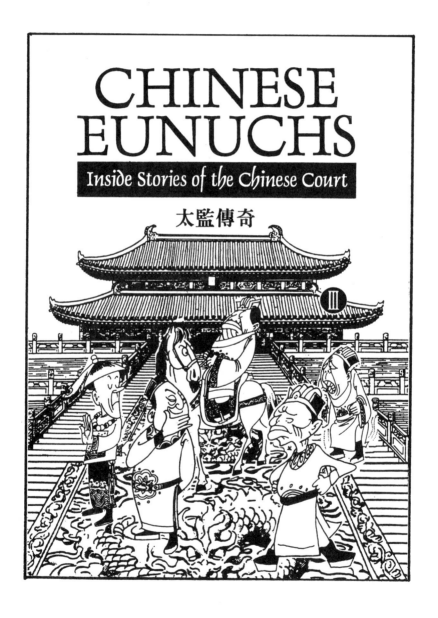

Asiapac's Latest Title

100 Series Art Album

Other Asiapac Titles

ASIA PACIFIC HERITAGE SERIES
A Dream of Red Mansions
Cast Your Chinese Horoscope
Contemporary Architecture in Hong Kong
Contemporary Chinese Fables
Fascinating Tales of Old Beijing
Feng Shui
Folktales of Old Japan
Ghost Stories of Old China
Golden Ox and Other Chinese Comic Tales
Journey to the West
Li Sao - The Lament
Liaozhai Stories of Fox-fairies, Ghosts and Other
Marvels
Ming Shu
Myths of Ancient China
Outlaws of the Marsh
Strange Tales of Liaozhai
Tang Dynasty Stories
"True" Crime Cases from Ancient China
Wisdom Stories

CREATIVE WRITING
Anthology of Chinese Humour
Butcher's Wife
Celebrated Stories by Great Russian Writers
Chess King
Dark Secret and Other Strange Tales
God of Fortune
God of Television
God with the Laughing Face
Heroin Trail
Jokes, Riddles & Proverbs from Asia and the
    Pacific
Legend of Planet Surprise
100 Smiles from Traditional China
Posthumous Son and Other Stories
Shades of Grey
True Story of Ah Q
World's Best "True" Ghost Stories
World's Strangest "True" Ghost Stories
World's Weirdest "True" Ghost Stories

GUIDES & REFERENCES
Concise Japanese-English Dictionary
Legal Status of Singapore Women
Popular Chinese Idioms: Volume 1
Popular Chinese Idioms: Volume 2

《亞太漫畫系列》

搜神記

編繪：王宣銘
翻譯：丘惠芳

亞太圖書有限公司出版